P9-ART-503

DISNEY

·I CAN DRAW·

Magical Characters

DISCARD
Woodbourne Library
Washington-Centerville Public Library
Centerville, Ohio

Walter Foster
Jr.

© 2021 Disney Enterprises, Inc. All rights reserved.

Illustrated by The Disney Storybook Artists. Step-by-step drawings by
The Disney Storybook Artists, John Loter, and Greg Guler.

No license is herein granted for the use of any drawing of a Disney character for any
commercial purpose, including, but not limited to, the placing of any such drawing
on an article of merchandise or the reproduction, public display, or sale of any such
drawing. Any use other than home use by the reader of any such drawing is prohibited.

This book has been produced to aid the aspiring artist. Reproduction of the work
for study or finished art is permissible. Any art produced or photomechanically
reproduced from this publication for commercial purposes is forbidden without
written consent from the publisher, Walter Foster Jr.

Published by Walter Foster Jr.,
an imprint of The Quarto Group
26391 Crown Valley Parkway, Suite 220, Mission Viejo, CA 92691
www.QuartoKnows.com

Printed in China
1 3 5 7 9 10 8 6 4 2

MIX
Paper from
responsible sources
FSC® C016973

Table of Contents

Tools & Materials

You only need to gather a few simple art supplies before you begin drawing your favorite magical characters! Start with a drawing pencil and an eraser. Make sure you also have a pencil sharpener. To add color to your drawings, use markers, colored pencils, crayons, watercolors, or acrylic paint. The choice is yours!

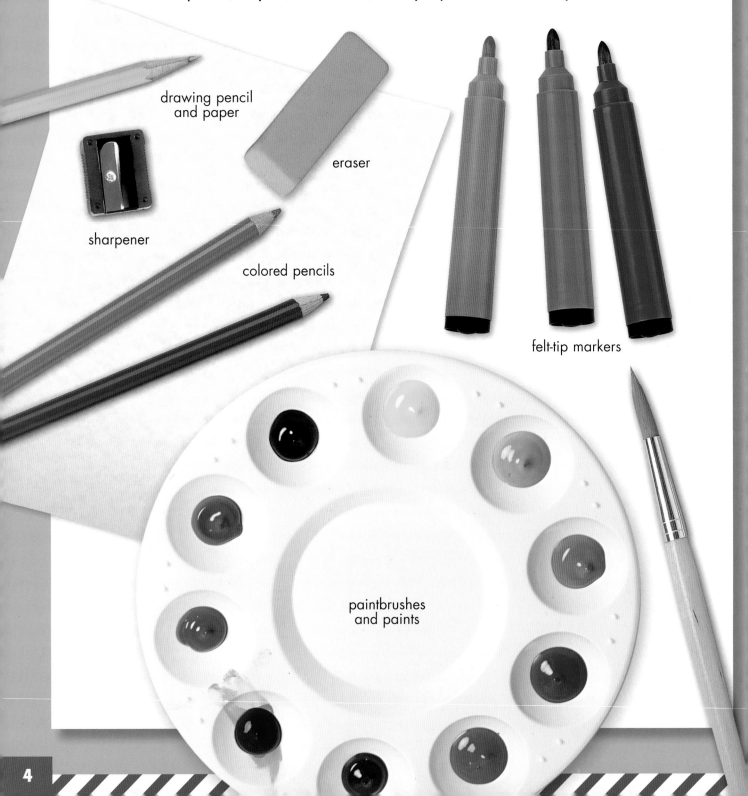

drawing pencil
and paper

eraser

sharpener

colored pencils

felt-tip markers

paintbrushes
and paints

How to Use This Book

You can draw any of the characters in this book by following these simple steps.

1

Start with a circle and guidelines.

2

First draw basic shapes using light lines that will be easy to erase.

3

Each new step is shown in blue, so you'll always know what to draw next.

4

Take your time and copy the blue lines, adding detail.

5

Erase your guidelines and clean up your drawing.

6

Now add color!

Sorcerer's Apprentice Mickey

Mickey is apprentice to the mighty sorcerer Yen Sid. Though his daily life is filled with magic, Mickey's duties revolve around humdrum chores, such as carrying buckets of water from a nearby well. One night, when Yen Sid goes off to bed, Mickey steals his magical hat and uses his power to cast a spell that will finally allow him some rest—or so he thinks.

When the tops of Mickey's hands show, be sure to add the stitching lines to his gloves!

Mickey's eyebrows can show how he's feeling

You can always see both of Mickey's ears,
no matter which direction his head is turned

4

5

Pinocchio

The wooden puppet, Pinocchio, is brought to life by the Blue Fairy one night after his creator, Geppetto, wishes upon a star for a child. Although he has a loving father and a "conscience" in a trustworthy cricket named Jiminy, he still struggles to make sense of right and wrong. If he can be brave and learn to be truthful, he stands a chance of becoming a real boy.

Jaq & Gus

Quick-thinking Jaq and clumsy Gus are good friends and make a great team, especially when it comes to protecting Cinderella and helping her achieve a happily ever after.

Flora, Fauna & Merryweather

These three good fairies—Flora (in red), Fauna (in green), and Merryweather (in blue)—protect Princess Aurora against the evil Maleficent and help Prince Phillip break the curse and awaken Sleeping Beauty.

1

17

The Cheshire Cat

The mischievous Cheshire Cat might be the maddest resident in all of Wonderland. Purple and pink stripes cover his plump body, and he has a wide, silly grin that never leaves his face. His ability to change his shape and fade into the background is fitting, because the Cheshire Cat doesn't quite seem to be "all there." He guides Alice on her journey through Wonderland, but he often speaks in riddles, perplexing sweet Alice and occasionally leading her into trouble.

Tinker Bell

Tinker Bell is a loyal and overprotective fairy
friend of Peter Pan. Wherever she goes, a trail of pixie
dust follows, and her voice sounds like the tinkling of tiny bells.
Tinker Bell's rounded pixie look is carried from the balls on the
tips of her toes to the little bun on top of her head.

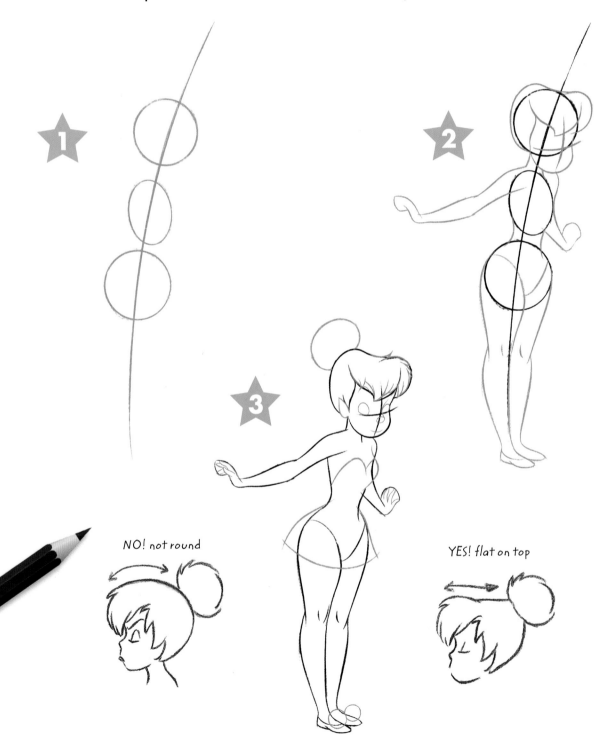

NO! not round

YES! flat on top

4

5

6

Mrs. Potts & Chip

With a spot of tea, Mrs. Potts can make any situation better. And her inquisitive son Chip keeps everyone's spirits up by shooting water through his front teeth.

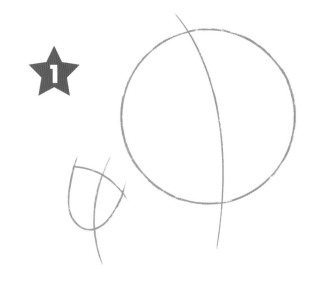

Mushu

Mushu is a tiny but mighty dragon and guardian to the Fa family. He was demoted from guardian to gong ringer after some past mishaps (he allowed Fa Deng to lose his head), but after helping Mulan save China, his guardian status was reinstated.

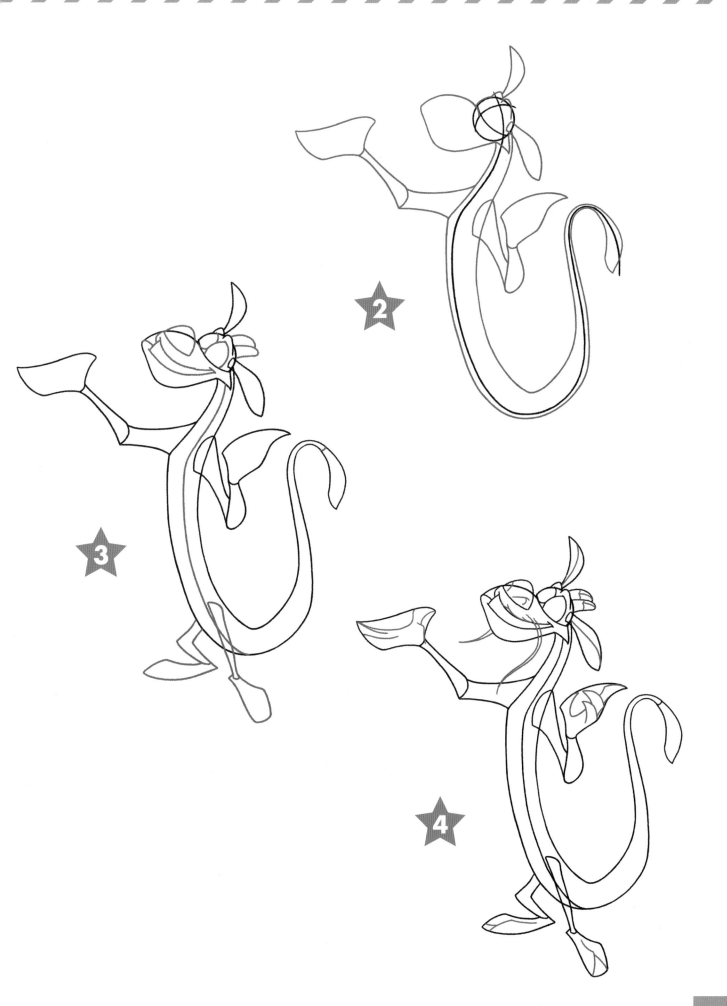

Olaf

Olaf is a curious and trusting snowman with a big heart. From warm hugs to summertime daydreams, Olaf is filled with optimism and happiness. He always sees the bright side of any situation and tries to help out whenever he can.

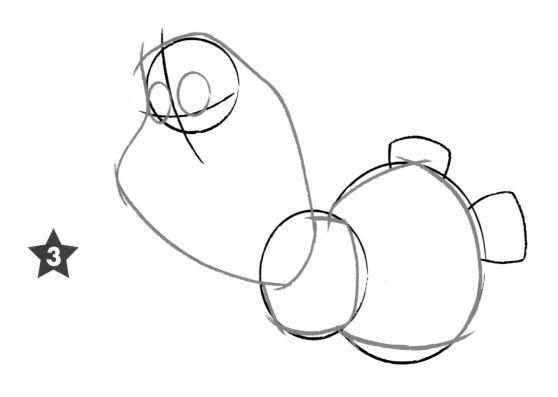

★ 3

★ 4

5

6

7

8

Also available from Walter Foster Jr.

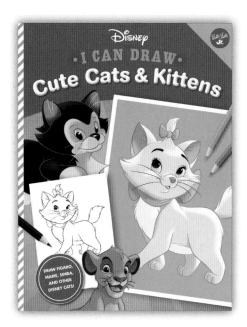

I Can Draw Disney:
Cute Cats & Kittens
ISBN: 978-1-60058-975-1

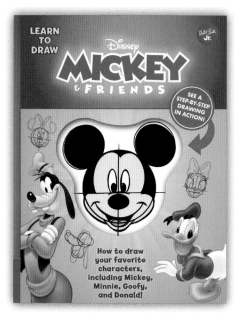

Learn to Draw Disney
Mickey & Friends
ISBN: 978-1-63322-655-5

Learn to Draw Disney
Celebrated Characters Collection
ISBN: 978-1-63322-672-2

Visit QuartoKnows.com for more Learn to Draw Disney books!